The Hard Life of a
and other Poems about
SEASONS

Compiled by Andrew Fusek Peters · Artwork by Kelly Waldek

First published in 2000 by Hodder Wayland,
an imprint of Hodder Children's Books.

This paperback edition published in 2010 by Wayland,
an imprint of Hachette Children's Books.

Wayland
338 Euston Road
London NW1 3BH

Wayland Australia
Level 17/207 Kent Street
Sydney NSW 2000

Editor: Sarah Doughty
Designer: Tessa Barwick
Cover Designer: Sarah Goodwin

British Library Cataloguing in Publication Data
The Hard Life of a Conker and other Poems about Seasons.
1. Seasons - Juvenile poetry. 2. Children's poetry, English.
I. Peters, Andrew (Andrew Fusek)
821'.008033-dc22

ISBN 9780750262934

Printed in China

Wayland is a division of Hachette Children's Books, an Hachette UK company.

www.hachette.co.uk

All Wayland books encourage children to read and help them improve their literacy.

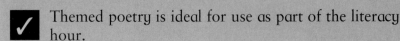 Themed poetry is ideal for use as part of the literacy hour.

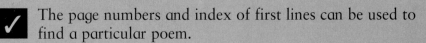 The page numbers and index of first lines can be used to find a particular poem.

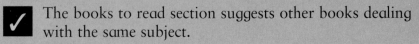 The books to read section suggests other books dealing with the same subject.

Acknowledgements: The publishers would like to thank the authors for permission to use their poems in this anthology:
'Frogspawn to Frog' © 1998 Penny Kent, first published in 'All Aboard, Secrets' (Ginn) compiled by Judith Nicholls.
'Rabbit's Spring' by Brian Patten by permission from Rogers, Coleridge and White. 'Snow On The Trees' © 1998 Jane Yolen.
First appeared in 'Snow, Snow', published by Boyds Mill Press. Reprinted by permission of Curtis Brown, Ltd. The rest of
the poems © and acknowledgement the authors.

Contents

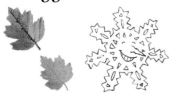

Spring Is Best . . . Or Is It?

In May,
when the sun comes out each day,
SPRING is my favourite season,
I say!

In July,
when it's even higher in the sky,
SUMMER is my favourite,
I cry!

In September,
when the conkers glow,
AUTUMN is my favourite,
I *know!*

In November,
I think of Christmas in December,
then WINTER is my favourite season,
I remember!

Judith Nicholls

The Morning Was Being Freshly Cleaned!

I sneaked past the front door
without it seeing me
only to be caught out
by the weather!

The morning was being freshly cleaned
and that included **me**!!

So by the time I had walked
all the way to school
I had been:

showered by a sprinkling rain,
brushed and scrubbed by an energetic wind
and dried out by a warming sun.

Indeed I'd been well and truly
spring cleaned!

Ian Souter

It's Spring!

Nests are packed.
Eggs are cracked.
Tiny birds
Begin to sing.
Like you and me,
They know it's Spring!

John Kitching

Rabbit's Spring

Snow
goes,

ice
thaws,

warm
paws.

Brian Patten

Aaaahhhh!!!! At Last It's Spring!!!!

James Carter

!!!!!!!!!!!!
!!!!!!!!!!!!!!!!!!!
!!!!!!!!!!!!!!!!!!!!!!!
!!!!!!!!!!!!!!!!!!!!!!!!!
!!!!!!!!!!!!!!!!!!!!!!!!!!!
!!!!!!!!!!!!!!!!!!!!!!!!!!!
!!!!!!!!!!!!!!!!!!!!!!!!!!!!
!!!!!!!!!!!!!!!!!!!!!!!!!!!!
!!!!!!!!!!!!!!!!!!!!!!!!!!!!
!!!!!!!!!!!!!!!!!!!!!!!!!!!
!!!!!!!!!!!!!!!!!!!!!!!!!
!!!!!!!!!!!!!!!!!!!!!!!
!!!!!!!!!!!!!!!!!!!
!!!!!!!!!!!!!

G
N
I
R
P
S
'
T
I
T
S
A
L
T
A

!!

H
H
H
A A
A H
A A
A A
A A
A A
A A
A A
A A
A A
A A
A

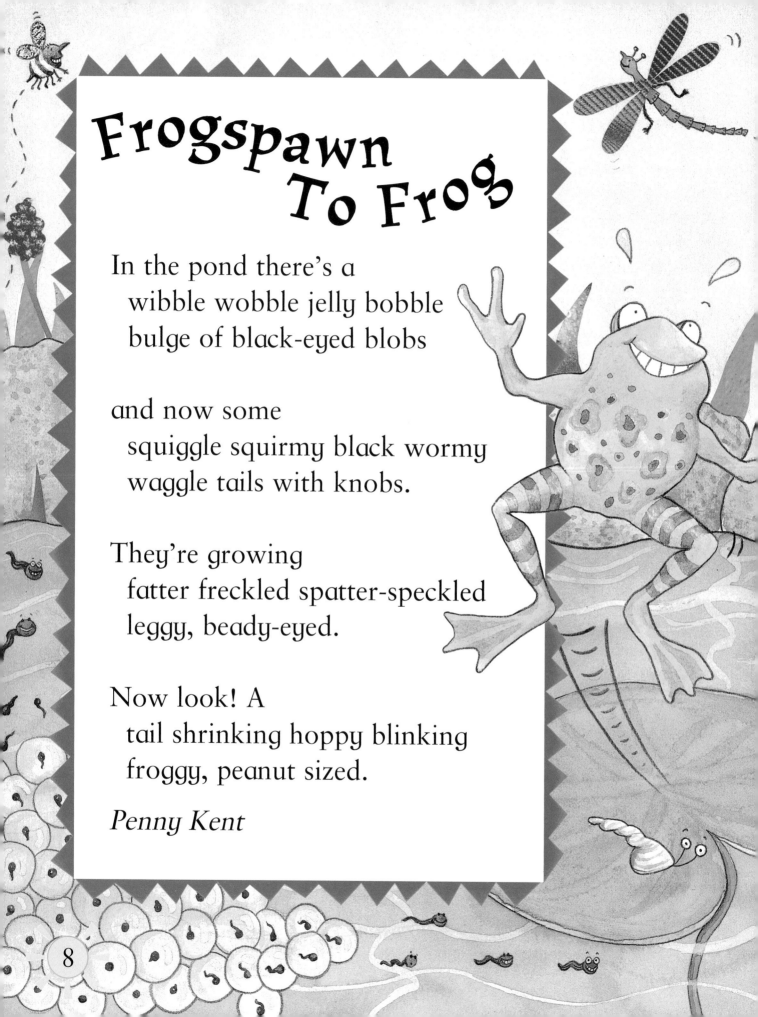

Frogspawn To Frog

In the pond there's a
    wibble wobble jelly bobble
    bulge of black-eyed blobs

and now some
    squiggle squirmy black wormy
    waggle tails with knobs.

They're growing
    fatter freckled spatter-speckled
    leggy, beady-eyed.

Now look! A
    tail shrinking hoppy blinking
    froggy, peanut sized.

Penny Kent

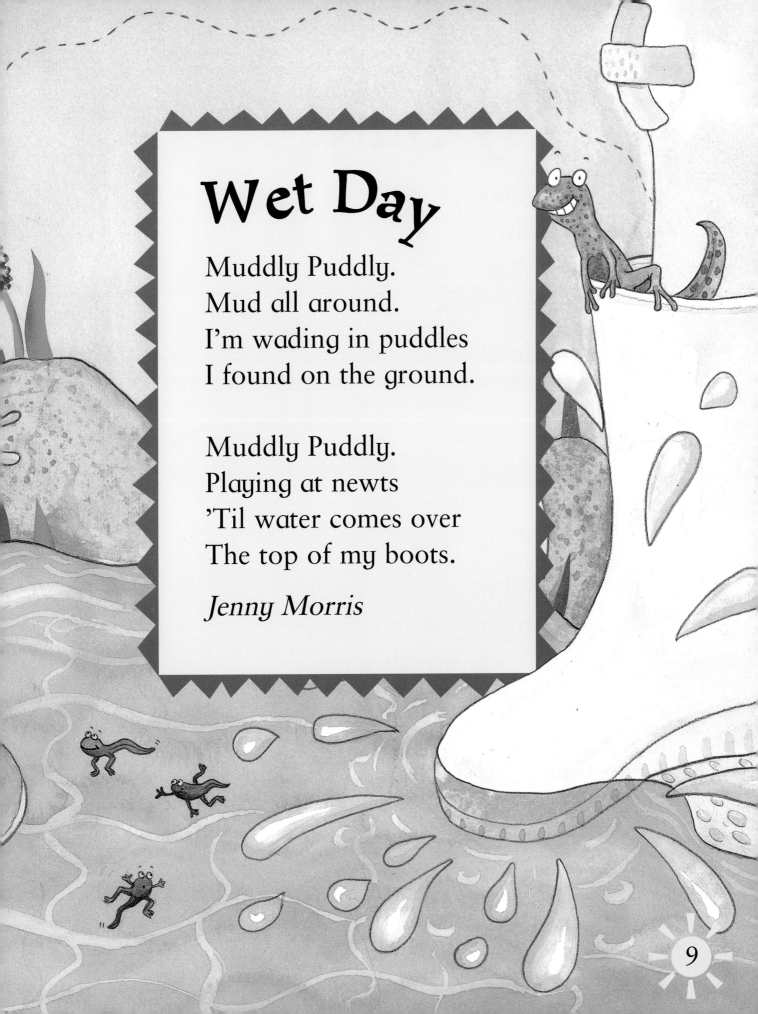

Wet Day

Muddly Puddly.
Mud all around.
I'm wading in puddles
I found on the ground.

Muddly Puddly.
Playing at newts
'Til water comes over
The top of my boots.

Jenny Morris

Peachy Sun

Hanging, golden,
Out of reach,
The sun like a
Tan talising peach.

Philip Waddell

July

Barefoot, holding wide-mouthed jars,
Trapping tiny twinkling stars,
July is when my friends and I
Bottle slices of the sky.

Bobbi Katz

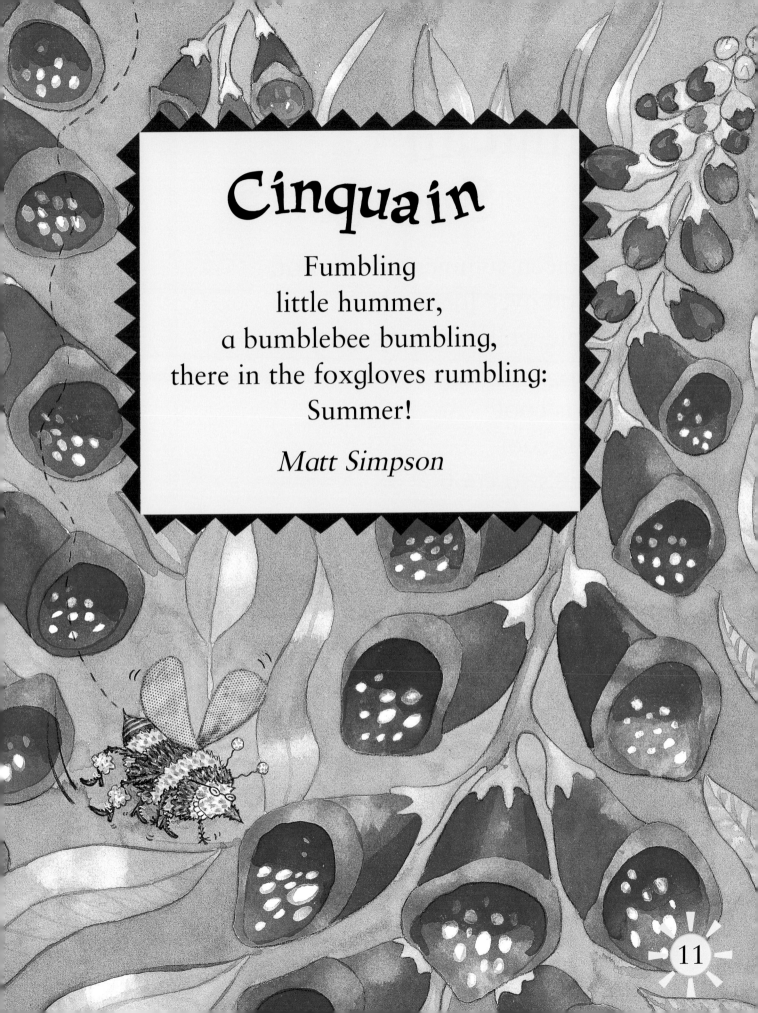

Cinquain

Fumbling
little hummer,
a bumblebee bumbling,
there in the foxgloves rumbling:
Summer!

Matt Simpson

Jamican Summers

Jamaican summers are so hot,
But all over Jamaica
People walk around saying
Dis is cool
Dat is cool
She is cool
Or he's so cool.

Jamaican summers are so hot,
Dat all over Jamaica
Parents are always saying
Drink yu coconut water
Drink yu kisko pops
Drink yu mountain water
Yu muss drink a lot.

Jamaican summers are so hot,
Dat all over Jamaica
People chill out in de shade
Sleep under trees
Or travel fe miles
To find cool breeze.

In Jamaica,
Very soon after summer
Come de winter,
But beware
Let me give yu a warning me friend,
Jamaican winters are so hot.

Benjamin Zephaniah

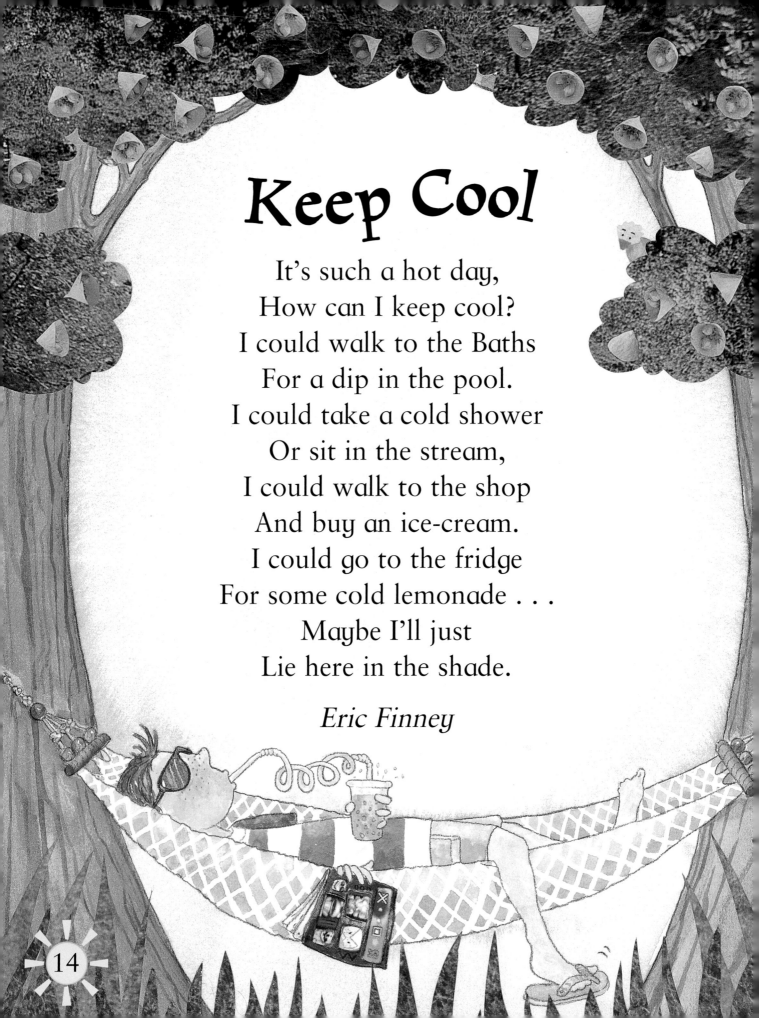

Keep Cool

It's such a hot day,
How can I keep cool?
I could walk to the Baths
For a dip in the pool.
I could take a cold shower
Or sit in the stream,
I could walk to the shop
And buy an ice-cream.
I could go to the fridge
For some cold lemonade . . .
Maybe I'll just
Lie here in the shade.

Eric Finney

What I Did In My Summer Holiday

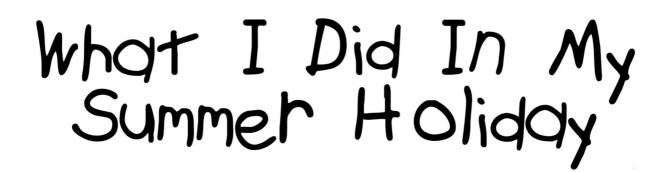

Oh, nothing much . . .

Climbed Everest one afternoon,
Went round the world in my balloon,
For England scored a last-kick winner,
Took Princess You-Know-Who to dinner;
Outgunned Clint Eastwood in a Western,
Reached the South Pole – without a vest on!
Shot Niagara by canoe,
Cycled from here to Timbuctoo;
Became a pop-star, topped the charts,
Transplanted half a dozen hearts . . .

Nothing really supercool.
I'm thankful to be back at school.

Eric Finney

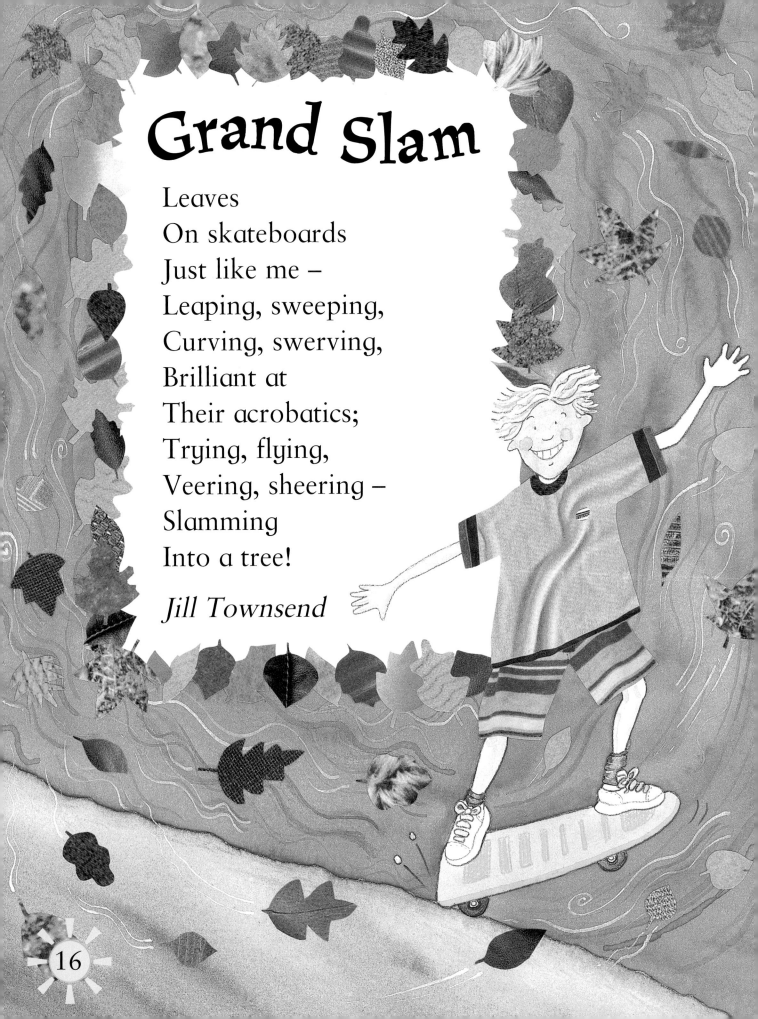

Grand Slam

Leaves
On skateboards
Just like me –
Leaping, sweeping,
Curving, swerving,
Brilliant at
Their acrobatics;
Trying, flying,
Veering, sheering –
Slamming
Into a tree!

Jill Townsend

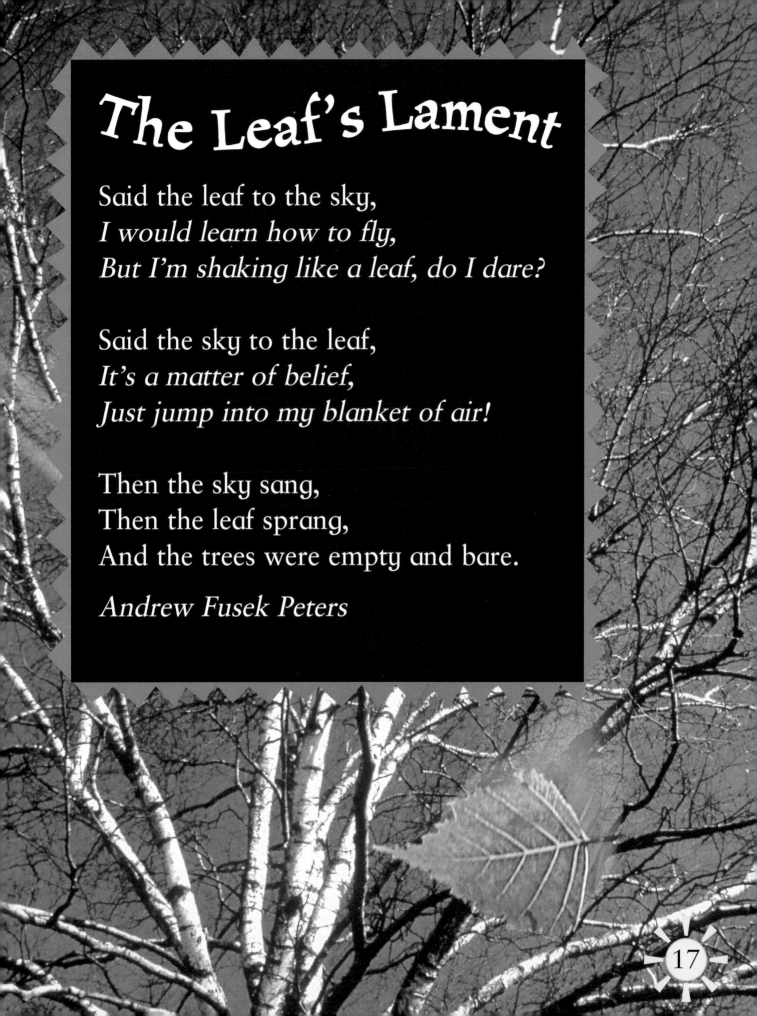

The Leaf's Lament

Said the leaf to the sky,
I would learn how to fly,
But I'm shaking like a leaf, do I dare?

Said the sky to the leaf,
It's a matter of belief,
Just jump into my blanket of air!

Then the sky sang,
Then the leaf sprang,
And the trees were empty and bare.

Andrew Fusek Peters

Cousin Autumn

Summer packed her bags today
To take her annual holiday
She jetted off beyond our reach
To seek the perfect golden beach.
She left a cousin in her place,
A cheeky chap with ruddy face.
We saw him bring a paintbox too,
But didn't know what he would do.
You see, this strange, eccentric fellow
Is daubing trees in red and yellow!

Polly Peters

It's Only The Storm

"What's that creature that rattles the roof?"
"Hush, it's only the storm."

"What's blowing the tiles and the branches off?"
"Hush, it's only the storm."

"What's riding the sky like a wild white horse,
Flashing its teeth and stamping its hooves?"

"Hush, my dear, it's only the storm,
Racing the darkness till it catches the dawn.
Hush, my dear, it's only the storm,
When you wake in the morning, it will be gone."

David Greygoose

The Hard Life Of A Conker

It's sad to be a conker
Picked up from the ground in autumn
Hole drilled through your middle
String knotted so you hang,
Then Bang! Bang! Bang!
  Until you split –
     The end of it!

Ivan Jones

Limerick

A lad called Abraham Zonkers
Found the hugest and hardest of conkers.
But a girl who looked sweet
Soaked hers in concrete.
She conquered and Zonkers went bonkers!

Polly Peters &
Andrew Fusek Peters

Winter Winds

Scarves wrapped round our necks
Hands deep in our pockets
Winter winds roar and rattle
Like teeth shaken loose in their sockets.

Roger Stevens

Cold Coming

First frost
Stars the glass.

The ground's hard
And ponds lock fast.

Birds blunt beaks
Trying to drill through grass:

No food or drink
While the frosts last.

Jill Townsend

Snow On The Trees

Somebody painted
The trees last night,
Crept in and coloured them
White on white.

When I awoke,
The tree limbs shone
As white as milk,
As bleached as bone,

As white as wool,
As chalk, as cream,
As white as ghosts
In a white night dream.

Just one day past
They wore dark brown;
Today they wear
A diamond crown.

Somebody painted
The trees last night
With ivory paint pots
White on white.

Jane Yolen

27

Snow Tray

At last there's snow.
So off we go
with Mother's teatray.
Don't know what she'd say.

It's smooth and slides.
Just right for rides.
With room on it
for you to sit.

Then home for tea.
Mum says to me,
"Had a nice day?
Now where's that tray?"

Jill Townsend

Toboggan

To begin to toboggan, first buy a toboggan,
But don't buy too big a toboggan.
(A too big a toboggan is not a toboggan
To buy to begin to toboggan.)

Colin West

Further Information

After reading the poems in this book, you can ask for the children's own close observations of the seasons. These observations can be divided into areas such as colours, shapes, sounds and feelings. Ideas can be collated on the board, or written out on card to form a 'poet's corner' wall display.

Many of the poems combine observation and imagery. 'The Morning Was Being Freshly Cleaned' uses personification (as does 'Leaf's Lament' and 'Cousin Autumn'). After reading 'The Morning Was Being Freshly Cleaned' aloud, write the word ALIVE on the board. If the door was 'alive' as in the poem – what would it say? Think of responses: perhaps "I can't handle this weather!". What might the raindrops do? "They could tickle us". How could leaves move? "They could bungee jump". Develop the answers into a group poem.

'Aaah!!!! At last it's Spring!!!!' is a shape poem. Ask children about all the things that happen in spring. When each child has a sentence about the season they could write it in the appropriate shape (e.g. a daffodil, or a lamb) and make a picture with their words. This can be turned into a shapely display for the classroom.

If you have a wildlife area with a pond, take the class out and read 'Frogspawn to Frog' and 'Wet Day'. The first poem is rhythmic and filled with alliteration. After looking at frog spawn (or a photograph of frog spawn indoors), ask for some descriptive words (e.g. slimy, round, black) and see if they can add words beginning with the same letter (e.g. swimming-slime) to make a sound poem. You can also do this with 'Cinquain' – e.g. yapping yellow bees.

'What I Did In My Summer Holiday' is full of impossible feats. Who can make up the biggest fib?

'Peachy Sun', 'Grand Slam', 'Winter Winds' and 'Snow on the trees' compare snow, sun and leaves with other objects. Seat the children in a circle to play the 'like-a' game. If the sun is yellow, what else is yellow? It could be yellow 'like a lemon', or yellow 'like Dad's socks'. You can do this with any adjective describing season-related nouns. Encourage children to look for other poems about the seasons. They can be copied out and put on display with found objects such as leaves and conkers (but obviously not snowballs!).

These activities will promote and reinforce the suggested work at various levels in the Literacy curriculum.

About the Poets

James Carter is a writer and teacher. He writes poems for children and books for teachers. He lives in Berkshire with his wife and young daughter. His hobbies include playing the guitar, listening to music and going to the cinema.

Eric Finney lives in Ludlow in Shropshire where he also used to teach. He has written hundreds of poems about school. His best ideas for poems come when he walks over to the nearby hill-fort or when he sits on his back lawn under the big walnut tree.

David Greygoose lives in Halewood, near Liverpool. He writes poems about trees and birds and stories about playing football. He likes to ride his bike, play viola, grow lots of vegetables and walk with his dog, Marley.

Ivan Jones reads and performs his stories and poems in schools and libraries all over the country. His 'Zot the Dog' books have been made into a series for television. His books about the ghost hunter are now a series for the BBC.

Bobbi Katz grew up hearing jazz on the radio. Words and rhythms were her first playmates. She still loves jazz as well as classical music and plays the djembe (an African drum). Her favourite sport is basketball. Bobbi lives in New York. Her newest book is 'Listen! A book of Noisy Poems'. (Dutton).

Penny Kent was born in Surrey and at present lives in a little farming village in Bavaria with her husband, son and daughter. She has had poems published in a variety of children's books.

John Kitching lives in Sheffield, but travels abroad quite a lot with his wife. At home or abroad, he always has a book to read. He also carries a small notebook in which he jots down ideas for poems.

Jenny Morris has taught in different schools in this country and abroad. Sadly, she writes jolly poems, and happily, she writes miserable ones.

Judith Nicholls lives in a very old cottage in a Wiltshire Churchyard. Her poems are sometimes mysterious, sometimes funny, about animals, people – and much more.

Brian Patten comes from Liverpool, but now lives in London. He is one of Britain's favourite poets. Among his bestselling collections for children are 'Gargling with Jelly' and 'Thawing Frozen Eggs'. (Puffin).

Polly Peters lives in a Shropshire village with her sometimes-grumpy husband Andrew (the compiler of this book), and lovely daughter. She writes plays and books and is mad keen on garden design.

Andrew Fusek Peters has performed his poetry and stories in thousands of schools. His books include the 'Barefoot Book of Strange and Spooky Stories' and 'Sheep Don't Go To School' (Bloodaxe). He loves walking and fiddly gadgets.

Matt Simpson lives in Liverpool, where he reads, writes, does crossword puzzles, watches television and plays with his grandchildren.

Ian Souter lives by the sea in Hove with his wife and two children. He is a teacher and part-time writer and enjoys writing, sports, photography and reading.

Roger Stevens began writing poems when he was at school. His first poem was all about Judy his dog, who stole the trifle from the kitchen table at Christmas and ate it. Roger's hobby is juggling with oranges and words.

Jill Townsend lives with her husband and an elderly Scottie dog near a forest in Hampshire. She likes walking, listening to music and seeing operas.

Philip Waddell currently lives with his wife in Uganda. He recently spent two years in a Bangladesh hospital teaching woodwork, metalwork and English. He writes poetry for lots of books and loves singing, travel, and films with special effects.

Colin West lives in an old house which was once a laundry in Epping, Essex. He enjoys collecting books and making up poems and stories.

Jane Yolen, known as 'America's Hans Christian Andersen', has had poetry published for both children and adults. She and her husband live part-time in the USA and part-time in Scotland.

Benjamin Zephaniah lives in East Ham, London and supports Aston Villa F.C. He loves Kung Fu, running and is a vegan. He tries to write poems that are fun but they should also have a serious message. He is very concerned about racism, animal rights, pollution, and he believes that boys and girls should be treated equally.

Books to Read

The Pear Tree by Meredith Hooper and Bee Willey (Macmillan, 1998). A delightful counting book, reworking the Twelve Days of Christmas. It goes through all the seasons of a pear tree and the animals that live in it.

A Year Full of Poems by Michael Harrison and Christopher Stuart-Clark (OUP, 1997). A big, colourful anthology which divides the year into months with a mixture of classical and modern poetry, suitable for reading aloud.

All The Year Round, Poems Through the Seasons by Vince Cross and Robin Bell Corfield (OUP, 1997). A collection of traditional and modern poems for younger children in the form of a picture book. There are shorter rhymes for joining in.

The Shepherd's Calendar by John Clare (OUP, 1993). A classic nineteenth-century pastoral poem, chronicling country life through the year, with a useful glossary at the back. A beautiful book which can be read aloud or dipped into by the more capable reader.

Blackbird has Spoken by Eleanor Farjeon (Macmillan, 1999). One of our best loved children's poets and author of 'Morning Has Broken'. . . poems about seasons, school, friends, bedtime and magic.

Cupboard Bear by Jez Alborough (Walker Books, 1990). A rhyming storybook about a polar bear who discovers that snow has turned into ice-cream. Well written, colourfully illustrated, a feast of a read!

Picture acknowledgements: Wayland Picture Library p12/13; McCharles/Britstock-IFA 17; Tony Stone Images 25, 27.25 (Darrell Gulin) 27 Tony Stone Worldwide

Index of First Lines